SHAKE UP YOUR LIFE

30 STEPS TO POWERFUL BRILLIANT LIVING

CHIEF EMPOWERMENT OFFICER
JENNIFER KEITT

TJ COMMUNCATIONS INC.

For permission requests, write to the publisher.
"Attention: Permissions Coordinator," at the address below.

TJ Communications Inc.
1720 Mars Hill Road
Ste 8-253
Acworth, GA 30101
www.jenniferkeitt.com | www.keittinstitute.org

Printed in the United States of America

First Printing, 2015

ISBN 0-9711141-2-8

TJ Communications Inc.
1720 Mars Hill Road
Ste 8-253
Acworth, GA 30101

CONTENTS

CONTENTS

SHAKE UP YOUR LIFE

PREFACE

I discovered my passion for doing what I'm currently doing now by accident. The year was 1991. I had been doing broadcast news for several years and had found myself in a very dark place one day as I walked into the newsroom. That day, I just knew. I knew that I could not do news for the rest of my life! I immediately got scared. I thought, "You can't be 27-years-old, and done with your career!" I had worked hard, graduated and got a job in my field. I had done 'everything' right and yet I stood there that day knowing I hated where I was in my career. And that sent me into a tailspin into dark chaos. That day I began to "shake up" my life.

A picture of the Chinese symbol for chaos hangs in the bathroom of my home. It reads, "Before the beginning of great brilliance, there must be chaos. Before a brilliant person begins something great, they must look foolish to the crowd." Shaking up your life looks crazy to everyone else! Why? Because passion costs, your dreams cost. And the payment for shaking up your life—moving from chaos to brilliance—will demand that you look foolish to everyone else.

Have you ever looked at a bottle of Italian salad dressing? If that bottle has been sitting for a while, before you pour it on your salad, you do what? You shake it up. You shake it up because all of the good, juicy herbs have settled to the bottom of the bottle. In order to get the richness of the dressing onto your salad, you shake up the bottle mixing up all the juicy stuff inside the bottle, bringing the flavors together. This is the same thing we've got to do with our lives from time-to-time!

I learned in Chicago all of those years ago how to shake up my life. Out of that dark place during that time came my future—my passion. All of the juicy parts of my life had to be shaken because they had settled at the bottom of the bottle of my life. The very thing that poured out of my life during that shaking is what I now realize as my purpose, my destiny, and my dream that I will continue to walk out for the remainder of my life.

The problem that the majority of us have in living the kind of lives that we want is that we don't want to look foolish to the crowd. My reality was that I looked extremely foolish re-evaluating my career choice as a 27-year-old news anchor in the third largest market in the country. That looked foolish. I was scared. But out of that "shaking" time of introspection, and much, much prayer, I realized God had something different for me to do.

So I took stock and analyzed of all of my gifts and talents, and thought about what I wanted to do with the rest of my life. I stepped out of my comfort zone. I harnessed my power deep within. I accelerated my potential. I kicked self-doubt to the curb. I embraced change, utilized all of my resources and I planned, planned and planned some more! I shook up my life, and I have never been the same.

I didn't throw the baby out with the bath water; I decided to stay the course in radio, but I changed my conversation. I decided that I was no longer going to be a person that reported the day's news events. I was going to become a reporter of 'empowerment' for women's lives. And out of that shaking came my nationally syndicated radio show, "Today's Black Woman," and in the launch of that show I found my future, my hope, my purpose and my destiny.

Many of us sit in our lives, we fit in and we die—slow deaths—daily. We die, still full of our dreams, still full of our desires and still full of our passion. I am here to tell you, no more. Start shaking up your life today.

I don't have any idea who's waiting for you to show up and pour your freshly shaken life all over them, but I can guarantee you that someone is waiting for you. You see if I hadn't taken that first step some 20+ years ago deciding to broadcast empowerment to women, I would not be here with you now through this book.

I have come to the conclusion that everyone has an assignment. Everyone has a purpose. Everyone has a reason for being—something that makes them full, overflowing and able to give to others. Some of you have been where you are now for years. Some of you are like I was in Chicago. You're in a dark place. Or even if you're at the top of your game in your career, or in your marriage, or with the kids; even if the whole façade looks great to everyone else, maybe you still know (as I knew) deep down, there's something more. You've settled. All of the juicy fragments of your life have dropped to the bottom of the bottle and you need to shake things up.

So when the kids are gone, or you reach that ultimate salary, or you get that final promotion, or you buy that bigger house, or you start that ministry or non-profit, or you visit that far away, exotic location, then what? What can you pour your heart, your soul, your mind and your strength into 24 hours a day, seven days a week for the rest of your life? What can you do so that you die empty—having achieved everything your heart desired? That's what I want for you—dreams released, destiny discovered, lives transformed, lives shaken.

Let's begin our journey. It's time to shake up your life.

SECTION 1
STEP OUT OF YOUR COMFORT ZONE

STEPPING OUT OF YOUR COMFORT ZONE

One day I was sitting at my desk and I started imagining something pretty morbid. I imagined that I had just died. And the very next thought that I had after that one was, "Oh my goodness, I didn't get a chance to do so many more things!" I thought, "I didn't get a chance to say, 'I love you' to my children one more time. I didn't get a chance to say, 'I love you' to my husband today. I didn't finish my doctorate degree. I didn't have my 50-year- old birthday bash!" I thought that day, "I didn't get a chance to renew my marriage vows, or travel to Paris. And this is the biggest one; I didn't get a chance to build my lifelong dream of a retreat, a global institute for women." I realized sitting there at my desk that day I can't die because I wouldn't die empty. If I would have died that day, I would still have unfulfilled dreams and visions still inside me.

What about you? If you died right now what would you have not gotten a chance to do? You have to step out of your comfort zone right now!

I read an interesting article that talked about the weight of unfulfilled goals. It said that, "Obituaries are filled with stories of successes and achievements, but they never list the longed for things that remain unfulfilled in people's lives." I've got a question for you. If you keep doing for the next five years, what you have been doing for the last five years, where will you be? Will you be closer to living your dreams or will you be exactly where you are right now, except five years older?

I've realized over the years most of us talk ourselves out of living life on a daily basis. We say, "Oh, it's already too late!" "My dreams don't matter anyway." "Nobody cares about me." "That's not for someone like me." "I don't have time." "I could never be as good as [fill in the blank]" "It's been done before." "What would people say?" "I'm just wasting my time." But truth be told all of those lies are saboteurs in our life journey that are designed to keep purpose away from us and they're designed to keep us from living our dreams.

It's time to shake up your life by taking the first step out of your comfort zone. Where do you begin? You start by simplifying your life.

DAY 1
SIMPLIFY YOUR LIFE

"The blessing of the LORD makes a person rich, and he adds no sorrow with it." - Proverbs 10:22 (ESV)

Newsflash, life can be very complicated! One of the categories that Facebook used to have under the relationship status was"It's complicated." That's how I feel sometimes about life: it's complicated! Between raising kids, keeping a relationship together, working, friendships, trying to be a better person, it's tough. I know you feel the same way, which is why when we start shaking up our lives, I want us to begin with SIMPLIFYING things.

When I do cook, I love wonderful, simple recipes. You know the ones that have minimal ingredients and even fewer steps of preparation. In a 1-2-3 step approach, I'm in and out of the kitchen in no time.

I am suggesting that your life can be simpler. With fewer pieces to shake up, life is sweet. Maybe you can simplify your spiritual walk. Stop sweating trying to force your relationship with God into your schedule and just make it a point to "be" with Him every moment of the day through prayer, reflection and meditation. Instead of trying to keep up with the neighbors and your friends, downsize, right-size and live within your means financially. Put away the complications associated with trying to make others be who you need them to be. Accept differences and celebrate them, instead of letting the differences drive you further apart.

Simplifying your life is taking the time to make your approach to your life as easy as 1-2-3. But it will take time and intentionality. To simplify actually means to reduce our lives to the basic essentials. Be honest, what do you actually need to make your life complete? Does it really take the $60,000 car instead of the $30,000 dollar one to make you happy? How many shoes can you actually wear at one time? Does it really take all of them to make you feel good? (You may not want to answer that question on the grounds that it would incriminate you!)

Simplifying is that process of making life easier, more bite-sized, less overwhelming and less complex as we pare down for the purpose of focus, clarity and shaking things up.

DAY 2
START WITH THE BASICS

"If any of you needs wisdom to know what you should do, you should ask God, and he will give it to you. God is generous to everyone and doesn't find fault with them. When you ask for something, don't have any doubts. A person who has doubts is like a wave that is blown by the wind and tossed by the sea. A person who has doubts shouldn't expect to receive anything from the Lord" - James 1: 5-7 (GW)

So now that we've begun simplifying our lives, we are making room for what the shaking process will bring into our life. After you've committed yourself to paring back and evaluating what's really necessary you become ready to start with the basics for this new place in your life.

When I hit that place in my career in Chicago that I mentioned earlier, I had to simplify my life and then through that process I discovered that all I needed to focus on were the basics. Basics are the foundational building blocks that your life is built upon. All I needed was my husband, my kids, my passion and joy. The basics for me then were centered on those who were most important to me and remaining true to my own heart. You see sometimes in life we clutter up our lives with so much stuff that we forget what the basics are. We become consumed with the stuff, the bells and whistles of life, and we forget all we truly need is peace of mind and someone to love. And here is another newsflash: all that you need you probably already have!

When my oldest daughter graduated high school at her Baccalaureate ceremony, the headmaster of her school gave the address. He told the graduating seniors about a book that he had read. The premise of the book was "everything I ever needed to learn, I learned in kindergarten." He then proceeded to encourage the graduating class to remember to be kind and considerate of others in life. He reminded them to play fair and to remember and demonstrate all the other 'fundamental' courtesies and 'rules' that we all should have learned as children in kindergarten on the playground. I thought it was the most profound thing my graduating daughter could hear — "you already know the basics for life success, you learned them when you were 5 years old in kindergarten!" In other words he told them, don't forget the basics.

Deep down I'm betting you already know the basics for your life success; you know everything you need to in order to get your life on track.

DAY 3
SEE THE NEW YOU

"If someone listens to God's word but doesn't do what it says, he is like a person who looks at his face in a mirror, studies his features, goes away, and immediately forgets what he looks like. However, the person who continues to study God's perfect teachings that make people free and who remains committed to them will be blessed. People like that don't merely listen and forget; they actually do what God's teachings say." - James 1:23-25 (GW)

We don't need mirrors in our homes because we are always carrying around one huge mirror in our mind—it's the one we use to 'see' ourselves with. I'm sure you're familiar with this mirror. You look into it and depending on how much value you've placed on loving you—this mirror determines moment by moment how you view yourself, what you see yourself doing and your current outlook on life. This mirror is always reflecting what you think about you and how you see yourself.

In order to shake up our lives, we've got to pull out some glass cleaner and wipe the mirror in our mind, to ensure that we are seeing our reflection clearly. If your inner mirror is damaged, cracked or needs a serious cleaning it's going to be very difficult to see the new you once you've shaken things up.

So how do we know if what we see is accurate? Is what you see how God sees you? Now I know for some of you this is a very intimidating statement, because you don't feel "worthy" enough for God. But how He sees us is the truest representation of how we should see ourselves. The glass cleaner that you and I can use, is the cleaner of the Spirit of God who shows us just how 'fearfully and wonderfully' God has made us.

DAY 4
SAVOR YOUR VICTORIES

"My brothers and sisters, be very happy when you are tested in different ways. You know that such testing of your faith produces endurance. Endure until your testing is over. Then you will be mature and complete, and you won't need anything." - James 1:2-4 (GW)

Ah…the sweet taste of victory—like a cool drink on a hot summer's day—victory quenches our thirst and refreshes our soul. Funny how the slower you drink cool lemonade on a hot summer's day, the more you're able to savor its quenching power, cooling your body while tingling your taste buds. You've walked through simplifying your life. You've also re-oriented your life toward the basics and eliminated all the extra stuff that's weighing you down. You've even looked at yourself in the mirror and I hope you're starting to see a new you already. Now, in this next step, we're going to take the time to savor our victories so far.

I believe very strongly in the need to celebrate. We just don't celebrate enough in our lives. I believe every milestone to every minor victory needs to be celebrated. Savoring is like taking a sip of your life and celebrating how it's tasting as your shaking things up. Savoring allows you the chance to 'taste' how things are going so far. Do you need to sweeten things up a little? Do you need to add more spice?

When I was in Chicago all of those years ago, as I began shaking up my life, I savored the victories that I had up until that time. I 'tasted' how good journalism, radio and TV had been to me. I savored how good I had become in reporting and disseminating the news. I liked what I savored and the more that I took the time to 'taste' my life, the more I realized what I wanted to keep.

You can do the same right now. 'Taste' your life. Is it too sweet? Too sour? Does it need some spice? Maybe it's time to pour it out and start over again! Savoring life is a must—savoring OUR lives is paramount, especially if we want to shake things up.

JENNIFER'S THOUGHTS

"If things go wrong, don't go with them!"
- Roger Babson

During your journey this week, you've looked at some ways that you can begin to step out of your comfort zone. By simplifying your life, starting with the basics, seeing the new you and savoring your victories, you should be trying on new thoughts and ideas that will help you shake up your life.

DIG DEEPER

What was your major take-away from week one: Stepping Out of Your Comfort Zone? What do you need to eliminate right now in your life?

EXERCISE: HOW AM I?

Look at the seven core areas of your life and either write one word which clearly describes how you feel about each area of your life right now, or give each area of your life a numeric value on a scale of 1-5 (1: not good; 5: excellent).

ACTION STEP

Now that you have taken the time to rate where you are in each of your Core7, answer the following quetions.

What was your worst area?

_____

_____

_____

What will you commit to changing to tackle this area?

_____

_____

_____

What was your best area?

_____

_____

_____

What will you do to celebrate your success in this area?

_____

_____

_____

YOUR FAVORITE SCRIPTURE THIS WEEK

_____

_____

_____

SECTION 2
HARNESS YOUR INNATE POWER

HARNESS YOUR INNATE POWER

Harness means putting into action or service. When I think about putting innate power into action or service, I start by asking "What innate power do I actually have/possess?" Before you can put something into action, you've got to be aware of what you have. For you, I want you to ask yourself what innate abilities—strengths, gifts, talents—do you possess? What's lying dormant deep within?

If you don't know what you've got, you will never be able to access it's power. It's time to access those reservoirs of power and harness them—put them into action and service. Take inventory. Re-discuss with yourself what your hopes and dreams are and then inventory what 'goods'—what current gifts, talents, skill sets and enthusiasm you have lying untapped inside. Then HARNESS that power!

In this section, we are going to go through steps that will not only allow you to shake up your life, but these steps will also enable you to tap into your innate power. We forget that we are powerful beings because we are created in the image of an all-powerful God! And if God dwells in you (2 Corinthians 6:16), then it's not your own innate power that you are harnessing, it's His power and strength!

DAY 5
HEAL SELF-DEFEATING THOUGHTS

"For as he (she) thinks in his heart, so is he. . ." - Proverbs 23:7a (NKJV)

Remember the story of the little engine that could? I remember as a little girl turning the pages of that book, looking at the face of the little engine, with 'sweat' popping off his face, struggling to compete with all the sleek, shiny, brand new engines. I chanted his mantra with him, "I think I can, I think I can..." over and over again. Little did I know then that I was learning an important life lesson: as we think so we become. I thought I could then, and guess what? Because I thought I could do things then, I CAN do things now.

I've also since discovered that it's perfectly O.K. not to be great at everything, but we do need to be great at some things. Although you and I can't climb every mountain and compete with every shiny new model that comes along, there are certain things - activities, friends, gifts, situations— that are uniquely designed for us and if we think we can excel in those things, we can.

In order to shake up our lives, step five is being intentional about healing our thought life, so that what we are thinking is in line with who we are becoming. When we practice thinking self-defeating thoughts we limit our ability to shake things up and to soar. We've got to come to grips with what we want in our lives and WHO we want to become in our lives and at the same time we've got to let go of all the other thoughts that are not serving us well. Self-defeating thoughts keep us comparing ourselves with all the other sleek, shiny, brand new engines and keep us struggling up mountains in our lives.

Today, commit to step five and begin the process of healing self-defeating thoughts. Eliminate the old, junky thoughts and replace them with clean, new, empowering ones.

DAY 6
HEAR YOUR OWN HEART

"Behold, You desire truth in the inner being; make me therefore to know wisdom in my inmost heart." - Psalm 51:6 (AMP)

Have you ever been in a public place, like a restaurant, that was so loud you had to shout to talk with the person sitting right next to you? Remember how hard it was to hear (and understand) what the other person was trying to say? Noise—especially the wrong noise at the wrong time—prevents us from being able to hear. However, it's the noise in our own minds and heart that I am more concerned about, because that noise prevents us from hearing our own hearts.

Maybe your heart is saying — don't make that move, be careful in that relationship, or go for that promotion. But if you can not hear it, you may miss vital, critical information when you need it most. Noise reduction, especially tuning out the noise in our minds, is the first step toward hearing our own heart.

Our hearts serve as the production center for our entire life. Everything that we have and get in life first germinates in our heart. *"Keep your heart with all diligence, for out of it spring the issues of life,"* Proverbs 4:23 says. "Keeping" is tied directly to "hearing." When we keep our hearts, we become quiet enough inwardly to hear what our hearts are saying and feeling and thinking. God speaks through your heart, so as your life undergoes this shaking process, allow yourself the time and luxury to hear fresh and anew what your heart is really saying.

Remember, your heart is instrumental in all of the major movement and activity of your life.

DAY 7
HAVE PATIENCE WITH YOURSELF

"My brethren, count it all joy when you fall into various trials, knowing that the testing of your faith produces patience. But let patience have its perfect work, that you may be perfect and complete, lacking nothing." - James 1:2-4 (NKJV)

Let's start this step with this simple exercise: I want you to breathe. On the count of three, inhale. One, two three...inhale deeply...now taking a long cleansing breath, exhaling...good, blow out all of the tension and frustration. Now relax... I wanted you to do that exercise so you could clear your mind enough to give yourself a break. We are way too hard on ourselves! And the next step in the shaking up our lives process is to practice having patience with ourselves. Rome wasn't built in a day and our lives won't be either. I know you've disappointed yourself, let yourself down and haven't lived up to your own expectations. Welcome to the club!

So many times we are so busy beating ourselves up over the past, over bad decisions, over what went wrong, what could be better, and on and on and on, that we forget that forgiveness is not only applied to others, we've got to start first with ourselves. When we practice forgiving ourselves, we can then begin developing patience. Patience is a fruit of the Spirit and a virtue that MANY of us need to develop - like yesterday (I have both hands raised). When you are patient and forgiving toward yourself, you can walk through life less frustrated and disappointed. When you practice having patience with yourself, as you endeavor to shake things up, you won't be moved when things don't go exactly as planned.

The truth is, we want everything in our lives NOW. We want perfect marriages, perfect homes, perfect kids, perfect jobs, perfect friends, and perfect money and when we come up short (and we will come up short) we get anxious, we fret, worry and beat ourselves up.

Don't do that anymore, shake up your life by giving yourself permission to have patience, with you.

Having patience is saying I'm O.K. where I am as I strive toward becoming the person of my dreams. Having patience is taking life one moment at a time as you grow and change. It's being comfortable in the skin you're in, as that skin is growing, shedding, maturing, and evolving. Patience (once worked on diligently) will take you toward maturing, toward a place of rest, toward wholeness and completion unlike any other character trait can.

Practice patience every single day of your life as you continue shaking things up.

DAY 8
HELP SOMEONE LESS FORTUNATE

"Each of you as a good manager must use the gift that God has given you to serve others." - 1 Peter 4:10 (GW)

We've all passed the countless men and women on street corners, at stoplights and in public venues who hold up signs saying that they're in need of assistance. We've all dropped a few dollars into their hands, only to go on our merry way feeling good about ourselves for helping someone "less fortunate" than ourselves.

But have you ever thought that all of us have signs that we are holding up deep within our souls that say what we're in need, hoping that someone will notice? Maybe you're fortunate enough to have a roof over your head and food on your table, but deep down in your soul, you're holding up a sign that says "In need of esteem, will work just to feel better about myself!" What about the "I'm lonely" sign painted in red in our soul that says "will take anybody, so I won't feel lonely tonight!" What about the need that you have for peace, or love or connectedness in your life?

The truth is, every one of us on the planet stand in our lives flashing signs of need every single day, and we hope and hope and hope that someone would drop us a few "dollars" - a smile, acknowledgment, care or just the right words - to ease the burden.

You see helping someone less fortunate than you doesn't mean looking at the outward appearance of a person and deciding by how "in need" they look whether or not you will help . . . helping someone less fortunate could mean looking a co-worker in the eye and letting her know, "You're good at what you do," or telling someone important in your life how much they mean to you. It's taking the time to be sensitive to those around you who need what you have at that moment to give. Helping those less fortunate could simply mean waking up to everyone around you, seeing their "soul signs" and serving and filling those needs.

This is a major step in shaking up your life. Today, help someone less fortunate than you.

JENNIFER'S THOUGHTS

"Many great ideas have been lost because the people who had them could not stand being laughed at."

- Anonymous

This week's journey started with the encouragement to harness your innate power! The quickest, most overlooked way to gain power and momentum in our lives is to get our thought life under control. That's why this week's journey started with the step of healing self-defeating thoughts. I don't want you to take one step forward and twenty steps back because your thoughts work against you!

DIG DEEPER

What was your major take-away from week two: harnessing your innate power? What are your most destructive thoughts and what do you plan on replacing them with?

EXERCISE: I AM YOUR MASTER
THINK ABOUT THIS...

I can make you rise or fall. I can work for you or against you. I can make you a success or failure.

I control the way you feel and the way you act. I can make you laugh . . . work . . . love. I can make your heart sing with joy . . .excitement . . . elation.

Or I can make you wretched . . . dejected . . . morbid. I can make you sick . . . listless. I can be a shackle . . . heavy . . . attached . . . burdensome . . .

Or I can be as the prism's hue . . . dancing . . . bright . . . fleeting . . . lost forever unless captured by pen and purpose. I can be nurtured and grown to be great and beautiful . . . seen by the eyes of others through action in you.

I can never be removed . . . only replaced.

I am a THOUGHT.

Why not know me better?

ACTION STEP

Answer the following quetions.

What needs to change about your thought life?

_____

_____

_____

What will you commit to change starting today?

_____

_____

_____

YOUR FAVORITE SCRIPTURE THIS WEEK

_____

_____

_____

SECTION 3
ACCELERATE YOUR POTENTIAL

ACCELERATE YOUR POTENTIAL

It was my first time in Germany and my first time driving on the Autobahn. My husband and I thought it would be fun to test our speed limits on the German highway traveling at speeds never allowed here in the States. On my way from Stuttgart, I was having a good old time cruising at speeds in excess of 100 mph! I really thought I was moving until I looked in my rear view mirror and saw in the distance the flashing of lights from the car coming up on my rear. Flashing lights signaled – MOVE, I'm coming. And to my amazement, the car was on my rear and passing me, with speed, while I moved into the next lane. I never broke my constant speed, cruising over 100 mph. In a flash the car was out of sight and I thought, boy that car made me feel like I was standing still, even at those high speeds.

Acceleration is the change in speed over a given amount of time and sometimes our lives need us to press on the gas and accelerate. For years I have used a car as an analogy for our lives. Imagine the frame, four tires, two lights, a steering wheel, and an engine. I don't care if the car costs $250,000.00 or $10,000.00 if it's parked, you're going no where.

Accelerating your potential happens after you've begun assessing what your life is about (sections 1 and 2) and it's the process of getting into your life "car," starting the car up and pressing your foot on the gas. It's about moving, forward. How fast you go is up to you. Where you go is also up to you. This step in shaking up your life is important because it gets you thinking about movement and going forward toward the next level in your life.

Many times we find ourselves stuck in ruts or places of non-movement or worse, going backwards. Accelerating our potential is freeing in that we recognize we do have places to go, people to help and things to accomplish.

In this section, think forward momentum and movement. See yourself pushing the gas pedal of your life car and slowly and surely accelerating, down the block, around the corner, out of your neighbor and onto the open highway of life.

DAY 9
ACCEPT YOURSELF AS YOU ARE

". . . Woman, where are those accusers of yours? Has no one condemned you? She said, "No one Lord." And Jesus said to her, "Neither do I condemn you; go and sin no more." - John 8:10b-12 (NKJV)

"Neither do I condemn you . . ." words that brought this woman, caught in the act of adultery, much peace in her time of trouble. When we do the unforgivable, it's hard to imagine that there is a God Who loves us enough to work with us through our challenges, so much so that He doesn't hold it against us. This is an incredible thought that can bring comfort to our souls if we really meditated on its meaning. If the Lord Himself has the capacity to forgive us in the middle of our mess, then why don't we grow comfortable with accepting ourselves just the way we are?

We're forgiven.

Learn to accept yourself. Acceptance is willingly receiving something - so accepting ourselves is doing what it takes to receive who we really, truly are. Be O.K. with who you are and with what you are about as you grow. That the key to growth and change. Notice the Lord's words to the woman: *" Go and sin no more..."* As you are becoming the woman He has called you to be, accept that there's no condemnation as you commit to not staying where you are. Step nine in shaking up your life is accepting yourself as you are, as you are becoming who God's calling you to be.

I'll be honest with you, you will never be content with yourself if you don't know who you are. Think about it, it's very hard to be comfortable with the unknown. Too many people have difficulty accepting themselves, because they haven't done their homework, they don't have intimate knowledge of who they are and how they're wired. But I'm excited that's not you. You are shaking up your life! Take your time with this step and get ready to accept yourself as you are right now.

DAY 10
ACT LIKE YOUR LIFE IS VALUABLE

"A good woman is hard to find, and worth far more than diamonds."
  - Proverbs 31:10 (MESS)

Do you believe that your life is truly valuable? I mean do you honestly think that there is something substantial that your life brings to the table that others in this world actually need? I'd love for you to believe without a doubt that you are needed, appreciated and valuable. Your value is not based on what you have or what you've done. What gives you value is the fact that you are created by a God who loves you, made you, and wants what is absolutely best for you.

Our value is forged in the coal mines of our lives as God Himself digs us up, cleans us and eventually presents us to the world the diamonds He's made us to be. Now it's up to us to act like our lives are valuable.

Don't treat yourself any old kind of way. If you had possession of a diamond of great value, you would protect it and keep it someplace safe. That's the same way it can be with our lives. If we value who we are we are going to make wise decisions that keep our lives safe and sound. If we think that we are valuable we won't allow others to treat us poorly or we won't make decisions that will harm our bodies, minds or souls. If we truly understood the price that The Lord paid for us, we would hold our heads up high all the time and know that we are people of the Most High God. We would walk with purpose and confidence. We would talk with authority and dignity. We would act like children whose Father is a King!

In step number ten I want you to consider very deeply just how valuable you are and to begin to act like it.

DAY 11
ATTEND TO YOUR OWN NEEDS

"Beloved, I pray that in all respects you may prosper and be in good health, just as your soul prospers." - 3 John 2 (NASB)

If you've ever flown, you've heard the flight attendant say that in case the cabin pressure drops, oxygen masks will be released and if you are traveling with small children or someone who needs care, PUT THE MASK ON YOUR FACE FIRST, before assisting them.

This is an incredible life principle.

While dealing with a rather challenging personal situation recently a dear friend was giving me encouragement that was so accurate and to the point; but I knew I couldn't do it. I said to her, "I know that where I am right now requires that I put the oxygen mask on my face first, before I try to save someone else . . . but I just can't do it." She assured me that I could do it. I finally had to admit that I had no choice, I had to attend to my own needs first.

It's hard to rescue and save others when your own needs aren't met. For starters, what exactly are you going to give them? Attending to your needs is really being intentional about securing for yourself what you need to function, to breathe, to live, and to be at peace.

Put the mask on you first, and then help others.
In this step-attending to your own needs-it may feel like the most selfish thing to do. But if Jesus had to do it, how much more do you think we need to? The Bible says, *"Immediately He made His disciples get into the boat and go before Him to the other side, to Bethsaida, while He sent the multitude away. And when He had sent them away, He departed to the mountain to pray,"* - Mark 6:45-46. Recognizing when you need to be alone to recharge and rejuvenate will save you. Knowing when it's time to attend to your own needs will keep you from shouting and screaming and becoming frustrated with everyone and everything in your life. Stealing away moments for yourself is something that isn't an option in shaking up your life, it's a mandate.

Attend to you first, always.

DAY 12
ASK FOR WHAT YOU WANT

"If you abide in Me, and My words abide in you, you will ask what you desire, and it shall be done for you." - John 15:7 (NKJV)

Why is it so hard sometimes to simply ask for what we want? Why can't we just ask our husbands for the affection we need? Why can't we just ask our bosses for the raises we want? Why can't we just ask our friends for their care and concern? And here's the biggie: why can't we just ask God for what we desire?

I've found that in life, asking for what we want is hard for many different reasons, including:

- Not wanting to rock the boat
- Not truly understanding what our needs are
- Pride
- Not wanting to need anyone
- Not believing God will answer

Whatever the reasons are, we all WILL need to ask someone for something one day, and since we are shaking up our lives, why not make today that day?

Life isn't a solo task (in case you thought it was) and if we all need others in order to accomplish our lives successfully, we might as well develop the skill of gracefully asking for what we want (and need).

For those of you (like me) who love remaining in control and really are uncomfortable asking for help, be forewarned this will not be easy. The Lord helps us learn how to ask by outlining the process of asking Him for what we desire. He said, *"abide in Me, and let My word abide in you, and then ask..."* doesn't that sound so easy?

In this step, let's try it! Let's get bold enough to begin asking for our needs to be met. You know God has an incredible way of placing you in the right circumstances at the right time- usually just a little in over your head - so you may find that you have no choice but to ask others (and God) for what you need.

JENNIFER'S THOUGHTS

"Be yourself! Everyone else is already taken."
- Oscar Wilde

In our quest to accelerate our potential—showing the world how truly wonderfully made that we are—it's imperative that we act like our life is valuable. This week we've looked at accepting ourselves as we are, acting like our lives are valuable, attending to our own needs and we've learned how to ask for what we want. I hope you are starting to feel the shaking in your life!

DIG DEEPER

What was your major take-away from week three: accelerating your potential? What fuel do you need to regenerate and fill your cup?

EXERCISE: TAKE OFF THE MASK

Becoming mask-less is probably the scariest determination and move that we can make as women. Taking off the mask is a three-step process:

1. *I take off my mask to myself.*

    No more lying to myself. No more self-deception. I must be and remain honest with me all the time (Step 11: attend to your own needs).

2. *I take off my mask to God.*

    Lord, here I am . . .check me out. I give you permission to see me naked. Do you want to know something? NOTHING about you surprises God and there is nothing about you that God hasn't already considered. Yet, He chooses us anyway!

3. *I can then take my mask off to others.*

    After being real with myself and with my God, what can others do to you? If God is for you, who can be against you? It is much easier for us to show others and the world who we are when we're living transparently and authentically before ourselves and before God.

ACTION STEP

Answer the following.

What masks are you wearing (i.e. the approval mask, the busyness mask, the "I'm ok" mask, etc.)?

_____

_____

_____

Who do you wear these masks with?

_____

_____

_____

Why do you wear these masks?

_____

_____

_____

What will you do today to commit to taking off you mask(s)?

_____

_____

_____

YOUR FAVORITE SCRIPTURE THIS WEEK

_____

_____

_____

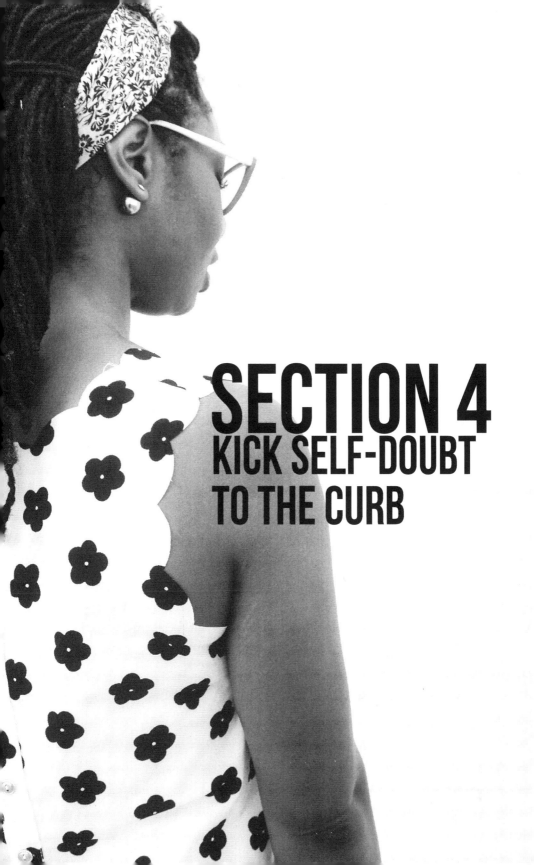

SECTION 4
KICK SELF-DOUBT TO THE CURB

KICK SELF-DOUBT TO THE CURB

I had been saying to myself for years that as soon as my last child left home for college, then it was going to be "my turn!" Like any good Mom, I decided that I would give each of my children all that I knew how to give so that they could have a fighting chance in life. I pushed toward the goal of getting them all to and through college, and as I write this book today, two have finished college and my husband and I have two more to go: one is a sophomore and the other a freshman in college.

I am now free to go for the things that I've put on hold for so long. But little did I know how "scary" it would be once life started opening up for me.

I still have to fight doubt!

As I'm writing this opening on "kick self-doubt to the curb" I am preparing to go on the Dr. Drew show. This is a national show that airs on CNN's sister-station HLN. Not in my wildest dreams could I have imagined having these kind of doors open for me, especially since for the past 25+ years I have been entrenched in raising kids and quietly doing my radio show. National TV exposure was always a dream but if I can be totally honest with you, I'm not sure I really believed it would happen.

As I was driving to the studio one day, I talked with the Executive Producer of the show and he said, "I think you have more in you, am I right?" Yes! He was right! I do have more in me, and as I write this to you, I am kicking self-doubt to the curb.

That's what this section is about, strengthening the relationship that you have with yourself even more, so that you can boldly go where you've never been before. That will start with kicking self-doubt to the curb.

It's funny to me how I still struggle with all of the classic fears we all have, "am I good enough?" "Can I do this?" "What if I fail?" But you know at the end of the day, I have to push past all of those negative thoughts and press forward, kicking self-doubt by the wayside.

And so do you.

The secret to kicking self-doubt to the curb is flowing in your gifts and talents and in areas in which God would have you to flourish— then going for it with all your might and strength. Let's delve deeper into this section.

DAY 13
KNOW WHAT MAKES YOU SMILE

"A happy heart is good medicine and a cheerful mind works healing, but a broken spirit dries up the bones." - Proverbs 17:22 (AMP)

When I was going through that tough transitional time in Chicago with my career decision, I discovered something. I had stop smiling. Somewhere between reporting all of the negativity that happened in the world, I lost my smile, and it was downhill from there.

During that period of introspection and reflection, I realized that being on the radio made me smile, ONLY if I was able to say something of substance and meaning that could help change people's lives. Radio still made me smile, but only when I was able to use my gift of communication in a positive way.

That took me down the development pathway that ultimately led to the launch of my nationally syndicated show: "Today's Black Woman." I had to know what made me smile.

When we are doubting ourselves, we're not smiling. Smiling is the connection to our heart that makes what we're doing worth it. A happy heart is like medicine; it makes you feel so much better.

It's very important that everyday of your life you strive to stay connected to what makes you smile and happy. Don't forfeit those things that bring simple pleasure and enjoyment in your life. Be intentional to stay happy— your heart, your mind and your life will love you for it.

DAY 14
KINDLE THE FIRE WITHIN

". . . But His word was in my heart like a burning fire shut up in my bones; I was weary holding it back, and I could not." - Jeremiah 20:9b (NKJV)

On cold nights, a blazing fire is intoxicating. To start a fire once it's grown cold isn't hard at all if underneath the ashes you still have embers glowing. All it takes is a rekindling of those embers to start the blaze all over again.

In life, we can grow cold. Cold in our attitudes, cold in our perspective, cold in our belief that we can make it, get it done or succeed in life. And sometimes we have to dig underneath the ash of failure, mistakes, doubt or hopelessness to find tiny embers that still may be burning.

Take a moment to search your soul...are there embers still glowing? If so, it's time to re-kindle them, put another log on the fire. Go back to the beginning, those first feelings, your first love. That's exactly what I did in Chicago before I found the path that has taken me directly into my purpose and passion. Go back to the core of what drives and motivates you.

I know the marriage may seem bad. stale, or dead; I know the job may feel like it's over; I know the kids are taking their toll on your sanity; you may even feel discouraged or caged in, but if you look closer there still may be some flickering under all that junk. No matter how small the embers, re-kindle the fire within so that you can burn and shine and warm up your life again.

DAY 15
KEEP A JOURNAL OF YOUR JOURNEY

"Guide my steps by your word, so I will not be overcome by any evil."
  - Psalm 119:133 (NLT)

There's power in journaling. Here are just a few reasons why you should consider journaling today:

- Increased awareness
- Sharper focus
- Creative problem solving
- Broader perspective
- Active thinking
- Empowers brain-storming
- Deeper level of analysis
- Stronger sense of self
- Generation of new ideas

- Clear the mind
- Life-changing potential
- Builds self-confidence
- Development of action plans
- Brings clarity of thought
- Greater honesty
- Self-paced learning
- Allows self-expression
- Integration of ideas and perspectives

- Uncovers unknown needs/wants
- Enhances self-expression
- Release of fears and tensions
- Awakens inner-self
- Stimulates self-growth
- Improved communication skills
- Better physical and mental health

But the biggest reason of all is that it helps you keep an accurate record of what the Lord has done and is doing in your life, proving His faithfulness to you! I'd like for you to take just a few moments and jot down some "ah-ha's" that you've discovered so far as you've begun shaking up your life.

_____

_____

_____

_____

_____

_____

DAY 16
KEEP BELIEVING IN YOUR FUTURE

"I know what I'm doing. I have it all planned out—plans to take care of you, not abandon you, plans to give you the future you hope for."
  - Jeremiah 29:11 (MESS)

Have you ever felt hopeless? It's not a good feeling. When I ran into the roadblock in my career in Chicago, I felt hopeless for a while. I felt like what's the use, I'm done, it's over. I stopped believing, briefly, in my future.

That was a dangerous place to be.

I had to shake things up and quickly start believing in my future again. The future is a powerful thing. It has this power to pull you, compel you and motivate you toward it but only if you believe in it. I love what God told Jeremiah, *"I have it all planned out...plans to give you the future you hope for.*" That's honestly, what began to pull me out of that dark space in my life, believing that I wasn't finished and believing in what my future could be and should be.

I took the Strengthsfinder 2.0 assessment (I highly recommend this assessment found in the book Strengthsfinder 2.0 written by Tom Rath) and discovered that one of my key strengths is that of being a "futurist." This strength allows me to see in detail what the future might hold. Stay with the shaking up your life process. Keep believing in your future. You have come too far to give up now . . . keep believing! What could your future look like? What should it look like? Begin to paint new pictures of a glorious, vibrantly rich future—YOURS!

JENNIFER'S THOUGHTS

"What would you attempt to do if you knew you could not fail?"
- Robert Frost

I hope you've done some serious damage to the obstacles that are in your life this week as we kick self-doubt to the curb! I want you to see yourself raising your foot and literally kicking that doubt out the door and slamming the door shut. This is also the week in which (if you haven't already) you grab a journal to take your experience with SHAKE UP YOUR LIFE to the next level.

DIG DEEPER

What was your major take-away from week four: kick self-doubt to the curb? What areas have you let grow cold in your life?

ACTION STEP: VISION BOARDING

Creat your own vision board!

A vision board is simply a representation of what motivates and excites you about your future. Take a large board and a stack of magazines and begin cutting out pictures, words, phrases, beautiful objects,etc. that represent the future you see for yourself. Hang it proudly in a place where you can see it and use it to keep believing in your future!

YOUR FAVORITE SCRIPTURE THIS WEEK

_____

_____

_____

SECTION 5
EMBRACE CHANGE

EMBRACE CHANGE

"Christians are supposed not merely to endure change, nor even to profit by it, but to cause it." - Harry Emerson Fosdick

C hange is happening all around you, right now: at work, with your friends, at home, and in your community. And when change happens, we always have a choice to make—stay where we are or change.

Author Robert Benson realized that he was ill equipped for life in this era and devised a theory of life that he calls the Rule of 21. He says, "twenty-one minutes is the amount of time that one can go without being interrupted by a telephone call, a knock at the door or an attack from cyberspace ...Twenty-one days seems to be the maximum number of days that one's life can go smoothly. The average is about four, but the limit is twenty-one. It's hard to live for more than twenty-one days without a car breaking down, a trip being canceled, a family member getting sick, a pet dying, a tire going flat, a deadline being missed, or some other thing that scatters all of one's otherwise neatly arranged ducks," he says.

Bottom line, ladies we must realize, understand and embrace the fact that CHANGE happens. And if we're going to shake up our lives, we've got to become very, very comfortable with change.

We must embrace it.

I have a sign hanging up in my office that reads: "Something's Gotta Change!" And I do believe that something, somewhere in my life must change if I'm ever going to end up where God wants me to be.

Change is an event that is situational and external to us. Change occurs when something old stops and something new starts. You are in the process of change right now as you read this book. Hopefully old ways of thinking have stopped and new possibilities have started. Change is happening all around you in your life. When you are facing change, it's helpful to step back and ask yourself the following questions:

- What do I have at stake that makes me hang in there in this changing situation?

- Who else in my world is affected by these changes in a significant way? (Think of all the people in your life.)

My life is in a change season right now. Not only have we become empty-nesters but my career is taking off in new ways and opportunities abound. I am asking myself, what's a stake in this change? What do I want during this change? And I am also evaluating carefully who's involved in my life during this change and how I need to keep them "in the loop" during this season.

Change is necessary, so we might as well stop resisting it and flow with it. As we shake up our lives, in this section look closely at the steps associated with embracing change: (1) expecting the best; (2) exercising discipline; (3) exuding enthusiasm and (4) encouraging someone else.

DAY 17
EXPECT THE BEST

"I can do everything through Christ who strengthens me."
- Philippians 4:13 (GW)

Brian Tracy said, "We will always tend to fulfill our own expectation of ourselves." And if this is true, we'd better expect the best. Expectancy is a feeling that something is going to happen; it's what you feel when you are expecting something. Question, do you feel that something positive is going to happen to you?

I certainly hope so.

I don't ever allow my children to slip in their expectations for themselves. I always encourage them to believe and expect that they will succeed, no matter what. When they do check-in calls with me daily, I talk to each of them about their "expectation" for the day, the week, the year, even their future. I keep them filled with positive expectations of being able to suc-ceed in love, in life, in their careers, with their friends and in this world. There is just too much negativity in this day and age and if we add to the negativity by expecting the worst to happen in our lives, how sad is that?

An expectation is a belief that is centered on the future, a good future. Now I'm not out of touch with reality, I know that bad things happen to good people, but when we expect the best for ourselves and about ourselves we are actually helping to craft and create a glorious future.

Shake up your life, by practicing step seventeen and make yourself expect the best in your life, your children's lives, your spouse's life, extended family and the lives of your friends.

DAY 18
EXERCISE DISCIPLINE

"And let us not be weary in well doing; for in due season we shall reap, if we faint not." - Galatians 6:9 (KJV)

Steve Pavlina writes a personal development blog on the Internet. He talks about the "five pillars of self-discipline." They are: Acceptance, Willpower, Hard Work, Industry, and Persistence. Pavlina says if you take the first letter of each word, you get the acronym "A WHIP" — a convenient way, he says, to remember them, since many people associate self-discipline with whipping themselves into shape. Interestingly enough, he talks about self-discipline being the ability to get yourself to take action regardless of your emotional state.

I love that thought.

We could all benefit from a course in discipline. I know this is easier said than done, but in the shaking up our lives process it is critical to our success. Discipline is that character trait that enables us to finish this process strong. It's just too easy to quit mid-way and say, I'm done. But that's true in our lives in so many areas. Dieting. Don't we quit after two days because it's too hard? Arguing. Don't we promise to keep our mouths closed and after two hours we've got something to say. Shopping. Don't we say we won't use the credit card but find ourselves buying something on sale "just this once!" And the list goes on and on.

Begin to look at your life critically. Know that hard work is the foundation and believe that if you are industrious you can begin to move toward disciplined behavior. Finally, understand, (as someone once said), that failure is the path of least persistence.

Let's get serious about shaking up our lives and commit to exercising the necessary discipline.

DAY 19
ENTHUSIASM IS CONTAGIOUS

"Rejoice in the Lord always. I will say it again: Rejoice!"
- Philippians 4:4 (NIV)

The word enthusiasm comes from the Greek, 'En Theos', which means the God within, being full of God, possessed by God.

Take a few moments and think about what you are enthusiastic (full of God) about in your life. In your family? In your career? With your friends? Are you practicing sharing your enthusiasm with those closest to you in your life?

Your enthusiasm is the sign of God within you to the world. That's why enthusiasm is so contagious and so easy to share. I dare you to get enthusiastic about this shaking process that you are in and begin sharing the God in you with others.

DAY 20
ENCOURAGE SOMEONE ELSE

"All of you set free by GOD, tell the world! Tell how he freed you from oppression..." - Psalm 107:2 (MESS)

I live everyday knowing that people are desperate for encouragement in their lives. Here's an email that I received this week from a young man. The subject line read: Help Me!

Good afternoon ma'am I just want to say that I read about you and I am writing today because I need advice and solutions on how to evaluate my life. Almost every plan I wrote and told myself has been crushed and didn't go into effect. It's like every time I put my hands into something, I end up messing it up. The bible said whatever comes out of a man's mouth might just come into reality, but sometimes I believe I'm cursed. I just can't seem to get my life together at all. I'm a father of a 4 year-old beautiful son that I'm away from because I'm trying to accomplish my dreams as a pro basketball player overseas. I am not just another black kid who's trying to just go to the NBA because he sees everyone else doing it. I'm very ambitious and believe that it will happen one day. I have lost so much as a 25 year-old young man every since I started playing ball in college and after college. I have lost contact with family members, time spent with my son and recently a relationship of almost

4 years. At just 25 years old I find myself depressed every day. I pray for strength to fight these tough times but it's so difficult. I have been disappointed so many times and let down that it's second nature. It recently got (more) difficult because a girl friend of almost 4 years is now dating (someone else) after our break up. I believe she left because she got tired of me not reaching my full potential of going to play professional basketball. At 25 yrs old I feel so lost and useless that I don't know what to do. All I have is a dream..and as far as being a father goes I feel like I'm letting my son down. Here I am broke, and insecure, barely able to take care of myself but yet I have a son. I'm in his life and will always be but I don't know what I'm doing. I feel lost, helpless, weak and afraid . . .

Have you ever felt like this young man? I know I have. I may not have had all of the experiences that he's had, but I know what it feels like to want someone to say "good job", or "you're good enough". His life definitely needs shaking right now and the biggest way it can be shaken is by ENCOURAGEMENT.

When you encourage someone you literally place courage back into them. It's a powerful process that can change lives. You can encourage someone with your smile. Encourage them with thoughtful words and deeds. Make it a point to encourage and build someone else's courage - to go on in life, to believe for better things, to fulfill their dreams and to take their lives to the next level.

After you've encouraged yourself, be sure to shake up your life by encouraging someone else too.

JENNIFER'S THOUGHTS

"What would you attempt to do if you knew you could not fail?"
- Robert Frost

There's a knick-knack decorative piece in my office that I look at every single day. It says, "Something's Gotta Change!" That is my mantra in life. Only those women who develop the skill of being flexible and ready for change will be able to survive in life. This week we're learning how to embrace change by expecting the best, exercising discipline, learning that enthusiasm is contagious and stepping out to encourage someone else.

DIG DEEPER

What was your major take-away from week five: embrace change? What do you need to do in order to get your discipline on track or moving at a greater speed?

ACTION STEP: ACCEPT CHANGE

Learn how to accept change in your life.

Taking the first step on any journey can be the hardest one. Too often, when dealing with change, we're expected to "just get on with it" to "think positively," and "go with the flow." But all changes have positive and negative consequences, new freedoms and new limits, new rewards and new risks.

1. Write some sentences that describe a single important change that you are facing.

_____

_____

_____

2. Now write down the top two or three positive and negative aspects of this change.

   •   Positive Aspects

_____

_____

_____

   •   Negative Aspects

_____

_____

_____

Now it's time to FACE change courageously. Maybe it's change in a key relationship, maybe it's financial, maybe it's emotional or even spiritual between you and God. Whatever the change is, I want you to answer the following questions:

1. What does this change really mean to me?

_____

_____

_____

2. How is it impacting me?

_____

_____

_____

3. What do I like about the change?

_____

_____

_____

4. What am I concerned about?

_____

_____

_____

YOUR FAVORITE SCRIPTURE THIS WEEK

_____

_____

_____

SECTION 6
UNLEASH YOUR MIND

UNLEASH YOUR MIND

I t's time to free your mind! As you shake up your life, the space between your ears is the single most powerful place to aid in your transformation. Your mind has got to be in agreement with the shaking that's happening in your life. It's time in this section to UN-LEASH your mind.

Everyday we have the opportunity to think thoughts. From the time our eyes open in the morning until they close at night, we are bombarded with messages given to us through TV, radio, texts, Internet, Facebook, Twitter, through our colleagues, bosses, friends and family. All of these sources are urging us to think thoughts: buy that brand, go to this restaurant, believe this or that about yourself or your work, live healthier, like me, friend me, help me, care about something, and on and on and on!

Question, when on earth do you have time to think about YOU and YOUR LIFE? When can you unleash your mind from everyone else's thoughts and start allowing your own thoughts to propel your life forward?

Now is that time!

Researchers say that the human brain produces approximately 70,000 thoughts on average per day. Now imagine that you unleash all of those thoughts to begin to work FOR you instead of against you. Envision each thought as a soldier that you control. At your command, you can unleash each thought to go to work on your behalf!

In no time, you will have an army of thoughts (about 70,000 per day) working on your behalf, helping you to shake up your life and move forward towards your goals and dreams.

That's what this section is about, unleashing your mind so that you can shake things up. I want you to start practicing unleashing your mind right now. The next two thoughts that you think – make them work FOR you instead of against you. Think "I can shake up my life and live the life of my dreams!" Good. Now let that thought march around in your mind . . . and now add some help to that thought. Think, "I can do all things through Christ who strengthens me!" Fantastic. Now let those two thoughts march around in your mind . . . unleash them and you will find slowly but surely you will unleash your life by shaking things up. Have fun with these next steps.

DAY 21
UNPACK YOUR POWER

"Trust in the Lord with all your heart and do not rely on your own understanding." - Proverbs 3:5 (ESV)

I love vacations, but I don't like packing. Getting the clothes, toiletries, shoes and stuff together is not my favorite task. But when I get to the hotel (on vacation) I do appreciate the packing process because I am able to unpack what I brought with me in order to enjoy my vacation. Guess what? If I didn't pack it, I can't unpack it and I won't have it on vacation.

This is an important life lesson: you can only unpack what you have!

In this step - unpacking your power - you've got to first take inventory of the power you possess. If you don't have anything "powerful" in the suitcase of your life, then you are stranded in life without what you need to succeed. But everyone has something powerful.

Start with your own inventory. What do you have in your life that is powerful? Your smile? Your wit? Your speaking skills? Maybe you can cook, or draw, or decorate? Maybe it's your award-winning personality or analytical ability? You've got to know what you have so that you can unpack it as you shake up your life.

Here's a list of words to get you started with your inventory. I want you to "unpack" your power by determining which six words on this list best describe you (or add your own). Once you know what you've got 'packed,' it's a breeze to unpack your power when you need it in your life!

Accurate	Confident	Self-controlled
Kind	Persuasive	Expressive
Adventurous	Creative	Self-starter
Leader	Physically fit	Good attitude Sense
Artistic	Curious	of humor
Level-headed	Physically strong	Hard worker
Assertive	Dedicated	Sensitive
Like outdoors	Practical	High standards
Challenging	Dependable	Sociable
Likes people	Productive	Imaginative
Civic-minded	Efficient	Stable
Loyal	Rational	Independent
Committed	Emotional	Tolerant
Original	Responsible	Inquisitive
Communicates	Energetic	Trustworthy
well	Responsive	Intelligent
Perfectionist	Entertaining	Intuitive
Compassionate	Self-assured	
Personable	Enthusiastic	

I AM

_____   _____

_____   _____

_____   _____

Of these six, select the three that represent your most prominent characteristics. Place a check next to them and get ready to unpack your power when you need it.

DAY 22
USE UPLIFTING AFFIRMATIONS

"What you say can preserve life or destroy it; so you must accept the consequences of your words." - Proverbs 18:21 (TEV)

Words create your reality. Because we are created in the image of God, like Him, we have this incredible ability to shape our world by the words that we use. Remember all that God said in the book of Genesis? He said, *"Let there be light,"* and *"Let the waters under the heavens be gathered together into one place..."* He said, *"Let Us make man in Our image, according to Our likeness . . ."* And you know the rest, everything that God said, He saw come into manifestation!

What would your life look like if you used those 70,000 thoughts a day and converted them into words that were affirming and positive? What kind of life could you create for yourself? 70,000 affirmations being spoken out of your mouth everyday, WOW!

In this step in the shaking up your life process, I'm encouraging you to use uplifting affirmations as a strategy in changing your life. I'm asking you to become super serious about every word that comes out of your mouth. I'm hoping that you will be so excited and hopeful about your life and future that you will help yourself by saying only positive things about you, your life, your family and your future.

Use these ten positive affirmations listed to get the ball rolling. Be sure to create your own and jot them down in your journal.

10 UPLIFTING POWER AFFIRMATIONS

- I see myself as exactly the person I want to be: confident, assured, healthy and prosperous.
- I walk and move with assurance, poise and power.
- I am fearless, courageous and bold.
- Everyday in every way I am growing more and more confident.
- I am confident, assertive and decisive in every situation.
- I receive wisdom and knowledge from God every moment of my life.
- I am filled with faith, certainty and hope in God.
- I am increasing in confidence, increasing my skills and abilities everyday.
- I take control of my internal images, dialog and feelings.
- I am now focused on the results I want and driven by passionate purpose.

DAY 23
UNDERSTAND WHAT'S AT STAKE

"You are the salt of the earth; but if the salt loses its flavor, how shall it be seasoned? . . ." - Matthew 5:13a (NKJV)

Have you ever tasted unsalted food? Not too good! It's interesting to me that when Jesus began talking about the importance of our lives, He chose to use the analogy of salt. We are the seasoning in our lives. We not only season those in our lives, but we are to extend our influence to the entire world. Jesus went on to say, *"You are the light of the world. A city that is set on a hill cannot be hidden" - Matthew 5:14 (NKJV).*

We matter. Our lives matter. We've got to understand what's at stake with this shaking up process, because after you're done shaking up your life, you'll be ready to be used for others.

The questions that I'd like you to start considering are "who am I here to influence? Who are the people that my life is connected to? Who might The Lord use me to 'season' or 'bring light' to?" We are all called and designed by God to help a certain type or group of people. Identifying the people you were specifically made to serve or bless is an important clue to your life purpose.

I want you to consider and answer these questions about who you want to help, so that you can understand better how important your life is and what's at stake in your shaking transformation.

Think of specific experiences, roles, or times in your life where helping people was particularly fruitful, fulfilling or seemed full of purpose. Reflect on these questions:

- What kind of people always catch my attention even when others don't see them?

- What kinds of needs am I consistently drawn to or sensitized to in those around me, in my community or even on the news? (Think people-needs not impersonal tasks.)
- What kind of people do I have a natural affinity for or want to hang around with?
- What kind of people am I helping now, or have tried to help in the past?

Once you've answered these questions, begin looking for patterns, and the common characteristics of the people you've been drawn to in your life. Remember, you must understand what's at stake in your transformation - their lives!

DAY 24
UNITE YOUR TEAM

"And when He called His twelve disciples to Him, He gave them power over unclean spirits, to cast them out, and to heal all kinds of disease." - Matthew 10:1 (NKJV)

You can't do your life alone. You need a team to support you. In this next step, you are going to think critically and carefully about those people in your life who are crucial to your life's success. Friends, relatives, co-workers, spouses, grown children, community members, all the people who you know in your life who may be vested in your success.

I want you to then pick a few key players and unite your team.

Think of these people as your personal board of directors. You can also view them as your personal consultants, or advisory team. You want to have diverse men and women, who you've given permission to speak into your life. Use them for their wisdom, their support and encouragement. Have them hold you accountable for completing the goals and dreams that you have.

Although great companies have a C.E.O. he or she does not run that company by themselves. They have others that help make the company great. It bothers me that people try to do their lives on their own, when all we have to do is ask and assemble help from others.

Assess who's in your life, and then unite your team.

JENNIFER'S THOUGHTS

"If we doubted our fears instead of doubting our dream, imagine how much in life we'd accomplish."

- Joel Brown

This week you are picking up steam as you move toward shaking up your life! I love the steps this week: unpacking your power, using uplifting affirmation, understanding what's at stake (this is HUGE) and uniting your team. I want you to really get serious about developing your personal board of directors. These are the people who are going to help you fulfill your hopes and dreams. They will be your accountability, your cheerleaders and your advisory board. They are essential to your life success.

DIG DEEPER

What was your major take-away from week six: unleash your mind? What are the common characteristics of the people whom you feel drawn to? Which are your favorite affirmations? What are your three power talents?

ACTION STEP: ASSEMBLE YOUR TEAM

Create a list of five potential team members. Write their names in the first column.

1. _____   _____
2. _____   _____
3. _____   _____
4. _____   _____
5. _____   _____

Next, determine what each person brings to the table. Why is this persona a good person to have on your personal board of directors? What do they bring into your life? Write what each person brings next to their name. Finally, commit to asking each person on the list to officially join your personal board of directors as you continue shaking up your life.

YOUR FAVORITE SCRIPTURE THIS WEEK

_____
_____
_____

SECTION 7
PLAN, PLAN, PLAN

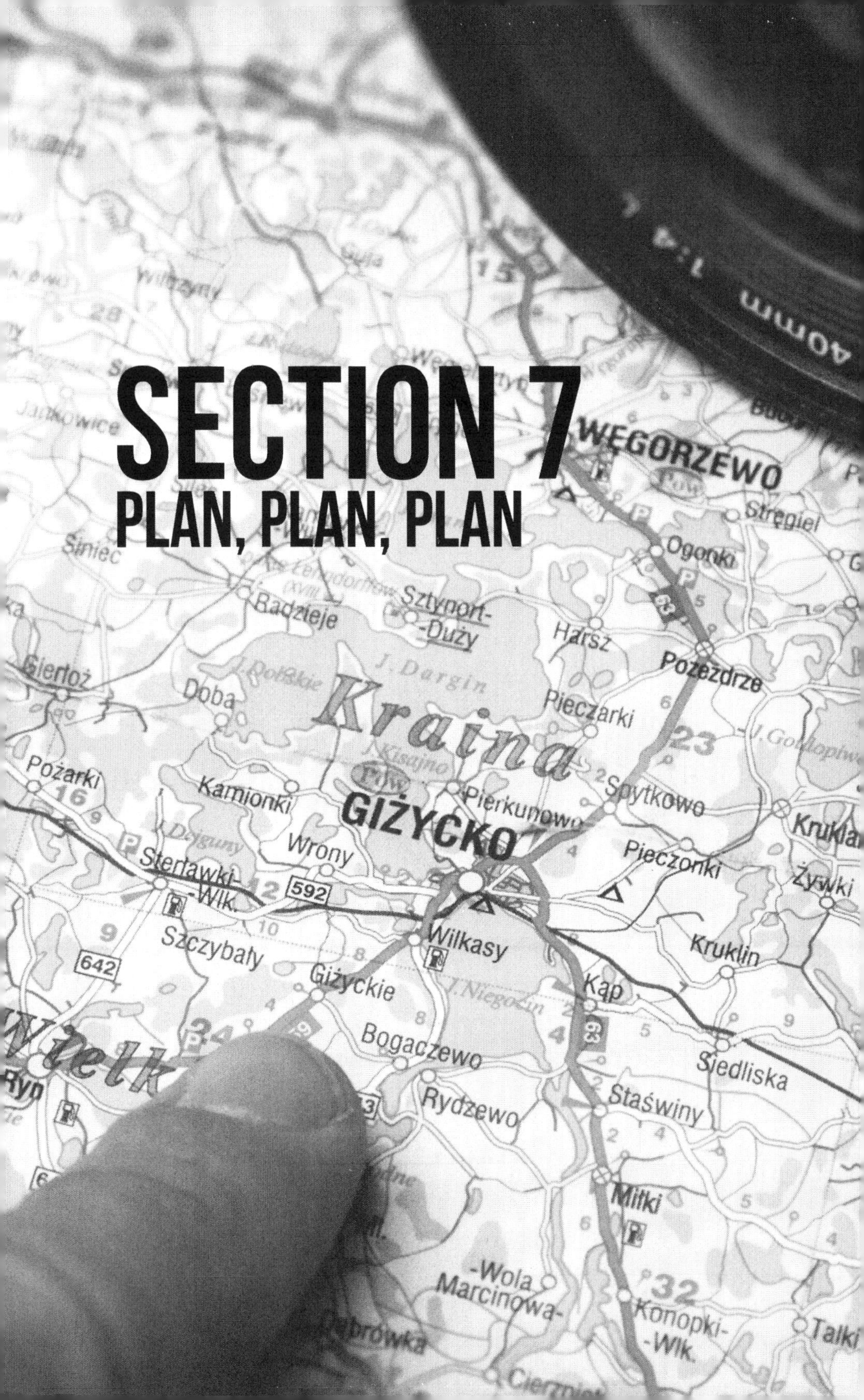

PLAN, PLAN, PLAN

It's time to get your plan together. You have come a long way baby! Now it's time to structure a workable, doable plan that you will use to complete the shaking process. This is the nuts and bolts practical section. This is where you sit down, think, plan, reflect, and begin writing down what you want to do with the rest of your life.

Here's what you are going to do in this section: *"Write the vision and make it plain on tablets, that he may run who reads it. For the vision is yet for an appointed time; but at the end it will speak, and it will not lie. Though it tarries, wait for it; because it will surely come, it will not tarry." - Habakkuk 2: 2-3 (NKJV)*

Have fun!

DAY 25
PREPARE FOR THE TRANSFORMATION

"Take a lesson from the ants, you lazybones. Learn from their ways and be wise! Even though they have no prince, governor, or ruler to make them work, they labor hard all summer, gathering food for the winter." - Proverbs 6:6-8 (TEV)

As a certified life coach, I am thrilled when I get the chance to have my clients do assessments. Assessments are your own thoughts about how you are doing in your life. Who better to assess you, than you?

In this step, we are going to prepare for the transformation by assessing where our life is. We're doing this now after all of the previous steps that you've taken so that you can be free and clear to start fresh and clean with the next level of your life.

TRANSFORMATIONAL PERSONAL ASSESSMENT

For each of the following sentences, mark how much you feel the statement is like you:

1: Very Accurate   3: Somewhat Accurate   5: Very Inaccurate

2: Accurate   4: Not Inaccurate

I have dreams and I am confident I will see them fulfilled.

5 4 3 2 1

I can generally see those things that keep me from fulfilling God's destiny for my life.

5 4 3 2 1

When I imagine myself stepping out and doing something radical, I am confident and can move forward.

5 4 3 2 1

I know where I want to go and am usually able to find the time, energy or money to follow through with going in that direction.

5 4 3 2 1

I am not a procrastinator. I know what to do, and I have no problem getting started.

5 4 3 2 1

I rarely spend too much time fighting fires, running errands, and doing urgent things,

5 4 3 2 1

I get right to what's important to me in the long term.

5 4 3 2 1

I usually have clear, written goals for the next month or year.

5 4 3 2 1

I have a structured plan to grow and make my life more significant.

5 4 3 2 1

How did you do? Reflect and share those items that you had the most trouble with. Then reflect and share on those items that you didn't have any trouble with. Prepare for your transformation, by honestly admitting where you are currently, what you need to work on, and then commit to developing a plan to get where you want to go.

DAY 26
PUT EVERYTHING IN PERSPECTIVE

"But my life is worth nothing unless I use it for doing the work assigned me by the Lord Jesus-the work of telling others the Good News about God's wonderful kindness and love." - Acts 20:24 (NLT)

Your life consists of many different experiences and stories. You didn't end up where you are by happenstance. In fact, where you are in your life is directly related to the circumstances and experiences and choices that you've made in the past.

As we shake up our lives, in this next step, let's take the time to put our lives into perspective. Let's discover how we got here.

As a coach, there's an exercise that I have clients do called "gleanings." To glean means to search something carefully. I have my clients search their lives carefully so that they can discover where they've been and how they've got to where they are. Once you know where you are, you've got half the job done. All that's left is to figure out your destination and develop a map to get where you want to go.

Use these questions to stimulate your thinking. Be sure to include specific experiences that seem significant to who you are and what your life has been.

CIRCUMSTANCES BEYOND OUR CONTROL. What positive or negative life circumstances have shaped you in fundamental ways? Include your birthplace, your upbringing, etc. that have helped define who you are.

_____

_____

_____

NEEDS. What kinds of needs (situations, circumstances or people needs) really tug at your heart? (Go back and look at the work that you've done in step twenty-three to help you answer this question.) What needs have you responded to throughout your life? What problems in the world would you want to spend your life solving?

_____

_____

_____

EXPERIENCE AND FRUIT. In what areas do you have valuable experience? Where has the most and best fruit in your life been? What kinds of things has your life experience prepared you to do? What have your negative experiences taught you about what you aren't made to do?

_____

_____

_____

CONFIRMATION AND COUNSEL. What have others seen and affirmed in you? Think of some specific events where you received significant counsel or feedback regarding what you should be about.

_____

_____

_____

GIFTS, SKILLS AND ABILITIES. What are you naturally gifted at? (Refer back to step twenty-one to help answer this question.) What important learned skills have you developed? In what kinds of situations do you really shine - where do your abilities really stand out?

_____

_____

_____

INNER KNOWING. What do you sense your destiny is? What have you always wanted to do with your life, maybe ever since you were a kid? What things do you want to do someday, that you're not even sure you'd want to admit out loud?

_____

_____

_____

FULFILLMENT AND DELIGHT. When did you do something that just clicked, that you felt born to do? What have you accomplished that was especially fulfilling. What are the little things in life that you just take a lot of pleasure in?

_____

_____

_____

REVELATION. What are the significant places where God has spoken to you about your life purpose? Do you have any specific destiny experiences in your life? What's the gist of significant times God spoke to you about your destiny or key scriptures you feel relate to your life purpose?

_____

_____

_____

These gleanings are what propelled me into my destiny back in Chicago all of those years ago. After I sat and thought about who I'm drawn to, and what my gifts and talents were and what my inner knowing was saying coupled with my experience and fruit, I knew that radio was still for me. I knew that I wanted my voice to impact and make a difference in people's lives. I knew that I felt drawn to women and that God had gifted me as a communicator. I had scripture after scripture that referenced God's plan for my life. And after a whole summer of contemplation, I decided to create "Today's Black Woman Radio Show," as a way to communicate a message of hope and empowerment to today's women.

It worked, and the rest is history. Grab your journal if you need more space and write out the answers to the questions in the gleanings exercise so that you can put everything into perspective as you shake up your life.

DAY 27
PRIORITIZE YOUR NEXT STEPS

"Trust in The Lord with all your heart, and lean not on your own understanding; in all your ways acknowledge Him and He shall direct your paths." - Proverbs 3:5-6 (NKJV)

It's time to develop a S.M.A.R.T. goal. Dreams are hopes that we might do someday. Converting a dream or objective into a goal is a decision to take tangible steps to pursue it.

We've been shaking things up for quite some time. And now it's time to prioritize our next steps. Goals are specific future targets that we are committed to becoming or accomplishing in an action-oriented, time-specific way.

Ask yourself, "Where will I be in 1 month? 6 months? 1 year and beyond?" You haven't gone through this shaking process for no reason. Prioritization starts when you choose one dream, one hope, one thing that you'd like to start the next chapter of your life achieving, being or doing.

S.M.A.R.T. goals are Specific, Measurable, Attainable, Relevant and Time-Specific. Look back through your shake up your life book. What thought, dream, character trait or area do you want to develop and flesh out in this next season in your life? Confer with your personal board of directors, what do they see you doing with your life? That's the thing that you'll want to develop a S.M.A.R.T. goal around. Write the goal down here:

_____

_____

_____

_____

_____

Make sure it meets the following criteria:

SPECIFIC: a goal is specific when you can describe it concretely to others.

MEASURABLE: you need to be able to tell when you've accomplished it

ATTAINABLE: it can't be a pipe dream or something unrealizable.

RELEVANT: a goal is relevant when it's important to you - when it references your values.

TIME-SPECIFIC: goals are not open-ended - they have dates attached.

Here's an example of a S.M.A.R.T. goal: "I want to get the training I need to start a home for unwed mothers in the next five years."

Let's move on to the next step.

DAY 28
PRACTICE WHAT YOU'VE LEARNED

"The wise woman builds her house, but the foolish pulls it down with her hands." - Proverbs 14:1 (NKJV)

Now that you have a S.M.A.R.T. goal written down, it's time to practice all that you've been learning. I want to make sure that EVERY goal that you have from now on you are able to accomplish in this next season of your life. So now that you know how to write a S.M.A.R.T. goal, keep practicing what you've learned by going deeper to flesh out that goal.

Let's say your goal is to build your dream house. The first step is to create a picture of what kind of house you are envisioning. See the house with your imagination. See your goal in its entirety! That is how you put to practice what you've learned.

Look at the goal you've said you want to accomplish. How will your life look when you've reached this goal? What is going to be different? What will you be doing? What will you say? How will you act? Talk through what your typical day looks like after you've achieved your goal. Picture your dream in detail: what is the ideal you are shooting for?

Paint the picture of your goal here by writing it down:

_____

_____

_____

You can do this step over and over and over with every goal that you want to accomplish. For extra enforcement, go back to step sixteen in the bonus exercise and pull out your vision board. As you believe in your future (step sixteen) you can couple that with painting the picture of the goals you have in mind by creating vision boards for each of your goals! The key now is to continue practicing everything that you're learning in this shaking up your life process. Be wise and continue to build your life, don't tear it down by not practicing what you've learned.

DAY 29
PERSISTENCE IS KEY

"I know your works. See I have set before you an open door, and no one can shut it; for you have a little strength, have kept My word, and have not denied My name. . . Because you have kept My command to persevere, I also will keep you from the hour of trial which shall come upon the whole world to test those who dwell on the earth."
- Revelation 3:8, 10 (NKJV)

Persistent people always get what they want. In fact, in Jesus' own words, He will reward those who have kept His commandment to "persevere" in this life.

If you've not been a persistent person in the past, it's time to learn how to be that way! Winners are persistent people. If you want to develop a winning persistent attitude ELIMINATE these words from your vocabulary:

- I can't
- If
- Doubt
- I don't think

- I don't have the time
- Maybe
- I'm afraid of

- I don't believe
- I (minimize)
- It's impossible

Now ADD these words to your vocabulary:

- I can
- I will
- I expect the best

- I know
- I will make the time
- Positively

- I am confident
- I do believe
- You (promote)
- God is able

In order to develop perseverance, you've got to maintain the right attitude when the going gets tough. You've got to realize that the rough weather will not last forever (but even if it lasts for a long time, you've got to be convinced that you can last longer and make it through!). The key to being persistent is to always have a game-plan.

In order to develop your persistence game-plan, I want you to take each of the ADD to your vocabulary words and write complete sentences in your journal that you can meditate on and repeat to yourself over and over as you are moving toward achieving your goals.

So for example, you'd take the first ADD words: "I can," and you'd write, "I can go online and fill out the application for college so that I can go back to school and get my degree." Do this for every one of the words or phrases, then refer back to them any time you are in need of a persistence boost!

Now there is just one more step left in this shaking up your life process. Read on.

DAY 30
PRAY WITHOUT CEASING

"In this manner, therefore pray: Our Father in Heaven, hallowed be Your name. Your kingdom come. Your will be done on earth as it is in Heaven. Give us this day our daily bread. And forgive us our debts, as we forgive our debtors. And do not lead us into temptation, but deliver us from the evil one. For yours is the kingdom and the power and the glory forever. Amen." - Matthew 6:9-13 (NKJV)

The one final and consistent thing that you can and must do when shaking up your life is to PRAY without stopping! Prayer is talking with our Heavenly Father. Good communication is the key to all intimate relationships.

When we are getting to know one another, we tend to spend more time than normal talking to one another. This holds true in our intimate relationship with God. We learn to recognize God's voice by spending time with Him in prayer. Here's how you can begin to recognize God's voice:

- God will gently lead and guide you (Psalm 18:35, 32:8; Isaiah 40:11).
- God will convict and offer the gift of forgiveness (1 John 1:9)
- God gives peace and a sound mind (2 Timothy 1:7).

Henry Blackaby in his book, "Experiencing God," says, "Prayer is a two-way fellowship and communication with God. You speak to God, and He speaks to you." He reminds us that what God says in prayer is far more important than what we say!

In this final step of shaking up your life, pray without ceasing. Remember that listening is an integral part of prayer and you want to make sure you take the time in prayer to hear what God is speaking to your heart. Praying without ceasing is simply keeping the lines of communication open with God at all times--day or night--so that you are constantly aware of His Presence, thoughts and ideas for your life. Blackaby says, "Prayer is a relationship, not just a religious activity."

Right now, practice praying by whispering this little prayer:
"Thank you Lord for helping me shake up my life."

Congratulations.

You're done. Your life has been shaken!

JENNIFER'S THOUGHTS

"Things turn out best for the people who make the best out of the way things turn out."
- Art Linkletter

What a journey! Thirty steps. Thirty thoughts to help you shake things up in your life! It is my sincere hope that as we've stepped out of our comfort zones, harnessed our innate power, accelerated our potential, kicked self-doubt to the curb, embraced change, unleashed our minds and planned for our redistribution that you have discovered how truly wonderful you are and why life is worth living! This week as we conclude this portion of our journey together, I want you to PRACTICE EVERYTHING that you've learned. Not just this week, but from now on in your life.

DIG DEEPER

What was your major take-away from week seven: plan your distribution? What is one S.MA.R.T. goal that you are now going after since shaking up your life?

YOUR FAVORITE SCRIPTURE THIS WEEK

_____

_____

_____

CONGRATULATIONS! YOU'VE SHAKEN UP YOUR LIFE!

CONTINUE TO MAKE SIGNIFICANT PROGRESS BY REVIEWING EACH SECTION EVERY 90 DAYS

EDUCATIONAL RESOURCES
FROM JENNIFER KEITT & THE KEITT INSTITUTE INC.

 www.jenniferkeitt.com

 www.keittinstitute.org

 www.jkpowerbreakfast.com

 Shake Up Your Life Workbook
available at: www.jenniferkeitt.com

 Unlocking Your Unlimited Potential
available at: www.jenniferkeitt.com

 Life on Track Curriculum
available at: www.keittinstitute.org

 Free E-Book: Red Carpet Ready
available at: www.jenniferkeitt.com

 thejenniferkeittshow

 +jenniferkeittshow

 jenniferkeitt

 @JenniferKeitt

 in/jenniferkeitt

 @jenniferkeitt

 jenniferkeitt